halse for hazel

Also by Frances Presley

The Sex of Art
Hula-Hoop
Linocut
Neither the One nor the Other, *with Elizabeth James*
Automatic Cross Stitch, *with Irma Irsara*
Somerset Letters
Paravane
Myne
Lines of sight
Stone settings, *with Tilla Brading*
An Alphabet for Alina, *with Peterjon Skelt*

Frances Presley

halse for hazel

Shearsman Books

First published in the United Kingdom in 2014 by
Shearsman Books
50 Westons Hill Drive
Emersons Green
BRISTOL
BS16 7DF

Shearsman Books Ltd Registered Office
30–31 St. James Place, Mangotsfield, Bristol BS16 9JB
(this address not for correspondence)

www.shearsman.com

ISBN 978-1-84861-340-9

Contents

for Tilla
in whose lens

halse

Driver, Dryslade, and Dyre were named in prehistoric times from an Indo-European word dru, which first meant any tree and specifically an oak. It would imply woodland where none remains.

—*from* 'Oak, ash and thorn' Hazel Eardley-Wilmot

Dru from drûto (Gallo-Latin) – strong, thick, close-set

dru

driver implies a wood
driving the word home

I was the driver
who implied a word on the moor

no other
cars on the ridge way

singing a reverb
is alive
did live
never died

in dry valley
they are drying
dyre lining
the earth

dru is a fine and dense rain
is hard pressed is
drastic
thick and close-set grain

there were woods
implying
that there could be again

halse

what of the hazel?

a clue appears in dialect
the reversal of sounds

invert some consonants
trans position

dyre for dry
crips for crisp

halse for hazel

e
lon
g
a
t
ing

pollen

crimson stigmas

loved vowels
a new and corrupt enunciation

reverse her sounds
reserve my suddens

palm

when thou pass est

through waters

a smooth trunk parts the words
fronds above
I will be with

thee

at the rootless base

a thee tree a three tree

we held crosses believed
to be palm

crayon a body on this tight woven parch ment
a limp doll
cupped in a small

palm tree an alien

fashion for a paved garden

without branches to cross

pin nate pen ed

through palms

can i pass

rood screen

not knowing
screened

rood pattern
open work

is

cruci
form of leaves

no cross bar
but cross wort

curves

has come down to us

space between
leaf contours

uneven symmetries
nothing can stop

the arch is exact
everything else

alters

King's Wood

leave to impark his woods and hills

a recognisable true tree
the endless spread

their endless break to the ground
          lost branches
                              fell aground   fell   bed

this crown is not the crowns
so little hair
          – I did not bother with a brush

leaf spots   yellow brown red
     will not leave
          oak serratives

sun cradled
shooting below
sparse branches

leaf spots   yellow   brown
     will not leave
          oak serratives

nails will naile on the pales if none be lost

a palisade to protect saplings
green plastic covers
          – I'd better get my waterproof

                              shed branches

                                        lifted off
                                                  hape   shape
                                                            gape
                                                  fissured
                                                          tail

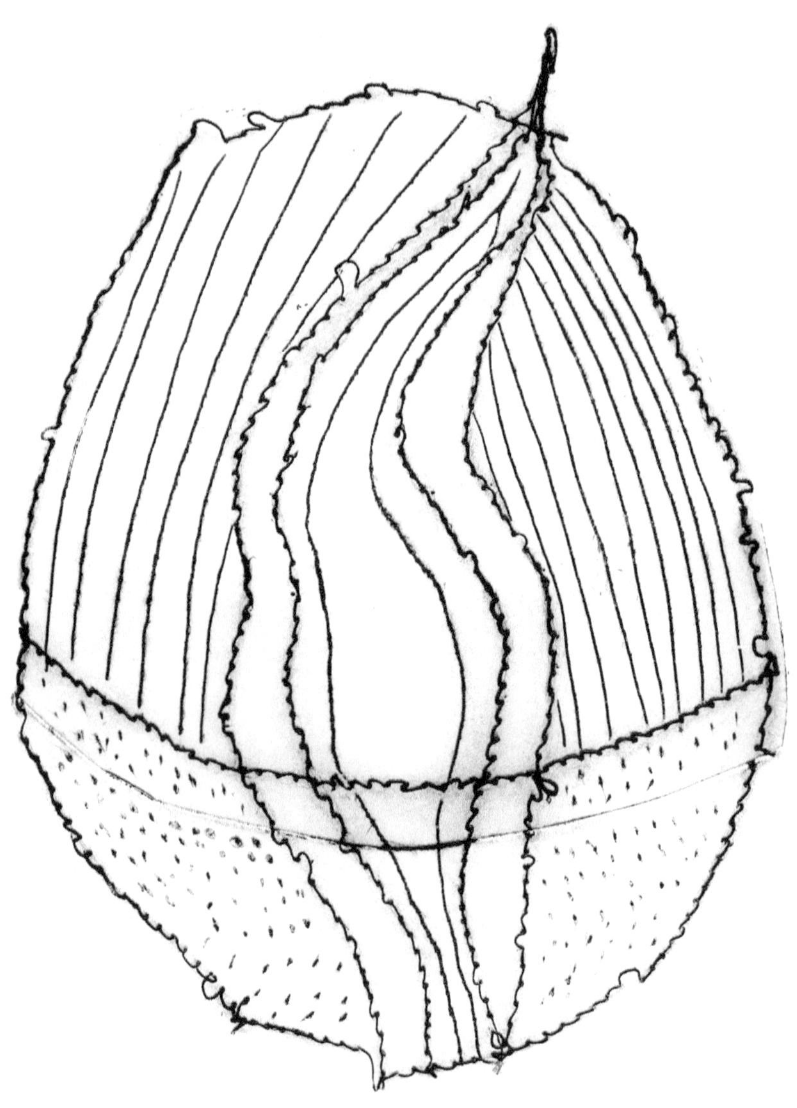

scrub oak

they were sending me down the wrong path and I had to follow a deer
track to cut back to the main path   so many fallen trees not the wood
we expect but brambles undo my laces branches fall again
all the plastic tubes the incubators fallen over   done and abandoned
the song of the saw
the slow painful labour of the bell   digital climb through the notes of
creation through the letters that I half remember
he is glad that Lovelock is glad that eight billion of us will
die it will be like World War Two and we will be happy to be in a war
but he says this will be an internal war fighting each other for scarce
resources and so
he is still glad not to be and cannot understand the contradiction in
Lovelock's position his brief optimism
and bird song   nor can I   present cross against a blue sky

if Lovelace was love less   what is love lock

scrub oak branches
twisted sort
scafrous burden

word is not penury
plenous overlay

bonobo nosewood
I can see my face
and my dear queen
it is not disagreeable

played like a keyboard
everything that points
travels   competes
and then is folded over

Bampfylde Clump (The Round Ring)

this turning turning of it
taken leaves
blown up
blown through

borne across
their talk
their saying
that they were saying

so many beech
blocked
beech clustered
dense but separate

fenced and speaking out
blowing out
circled round and back

taken over
offered levels
held forward   branches

height above height
to overcome
to overreach

the pasture

burnt mound

fractured

stones charcoal

waterlog
preserved

narrow combes streams move around
must have timber

beech hedge unbroken expect gaps
laid up let go
the width of the combe beyond the limit

pit heath

embrace

ac

hoar
har

ac
oak

mossed
twigs find
            outrange

          reached beyond strength

                    silver thrust
                              inter nodes

                    sent out to live
                                        on blue air

a green lichen exchange
bark takes back

                    roots
                                        at risk

Flitton Oak

soft orange
contours

no abri
or apricot

half roof
broken brain mass

ploughed bark
hard venture

long undulations
of rot

buzzard droppings

soft testicles

oakicules
he said

rowan

for my mother

white spindle
swallowed in red

plastic beads
string breaks

blood orange
clusters

they return to the tree
intact

Culvercliff

lichen not lost
crow croak

outstretch vetch
            sudden drop

white book?
               bark
birch

into hillside
out of

leaf mould materials
bromed and greened

a suspended branch
a slope that slips

aqua marian depths
between

these branches together made
an interlacing

where the furthest extent of
the furthest twig

until the branches already in bud
are so far down

and have forked more and never more vertical
holds

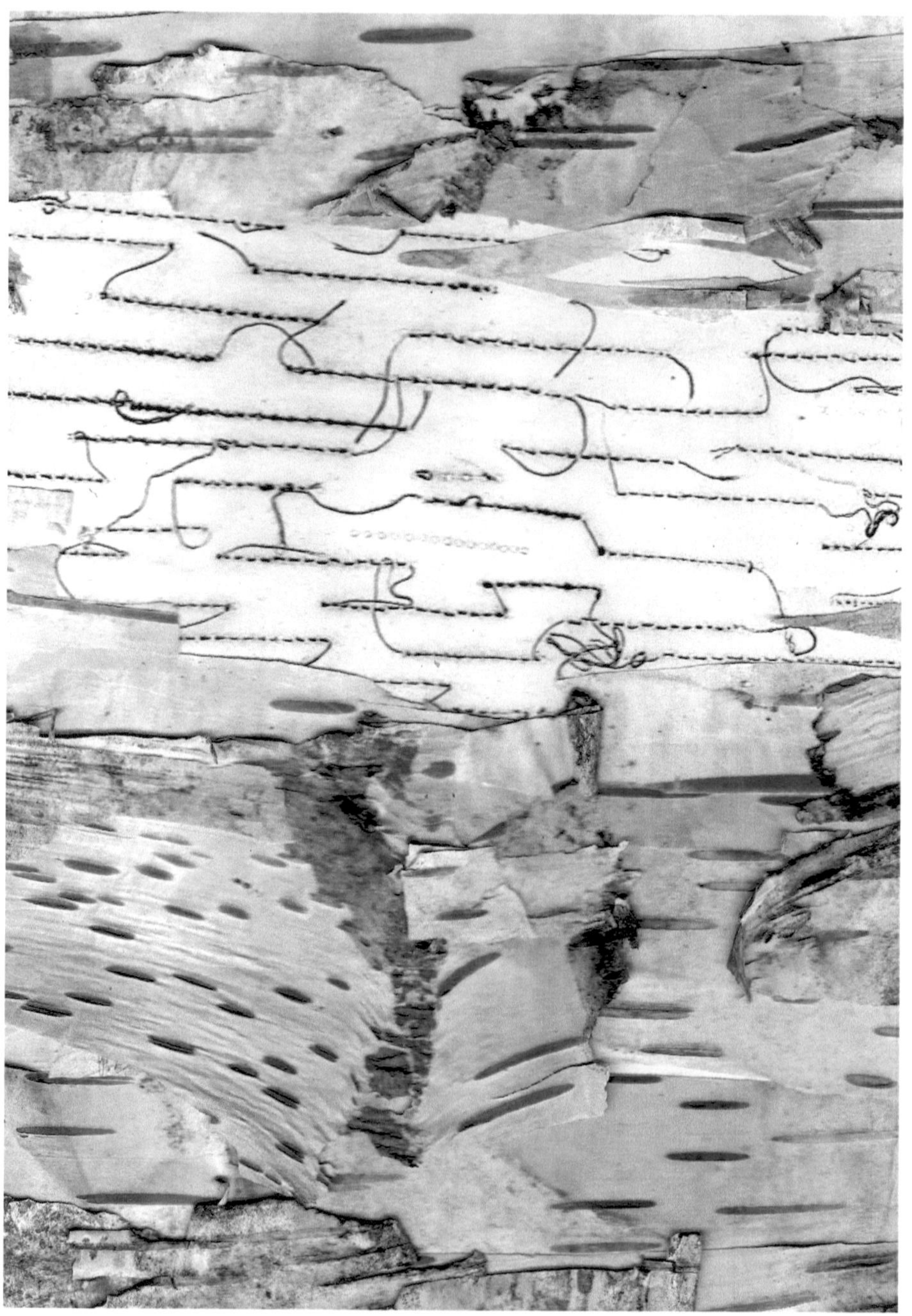

tank practice

I dreamt I was on Piccadilly again five hundred
thousand of us marching against the cuts funnelled
between the Ritz and the Royal Academy
I saw a car speeding through the crowd. Braking.
In front of me. The agonised face of the driver
Michael Foot
further down the track white stubs of roe deer
graze new grass and leaves

a military road built from end to end concrete turning places for tanks

resurfaced concrete

shadow of an ivied pine
dead yellow nettles

cast cuneiform wedges

what is this hard core
hard floor for?

no one in the Severn estuary

walk out
walk over to

nettled and dock dashed pebbles
bee subterfuge brambles

layer of brushwood green on white
mossed concrete

bury feet in dead leaves

soft bed for the lasts

tanks ploughed out the bracken ling dominates

pine

if the tallest pines
press close
find their places

who else is here
a plaintive cry
or just a calling cry

cries of irritation
a clash of pebbles
they're saying piss off

sightless
slightnesses
some stupid arguments

home killed
signed on the butcher's van
s(laughter)

lower branches snapped
a telegraph pole
of broken rungs

the base is only the base
but it is
buttercups

a patch of sand
flicks her ears
above the ferns

boll

is that the way I write?

there is no way
or this is it
below the bole

you are going on
and may be coming back

your ears are susceptible
when I thought nothing was

I dreamt that the bowl
was not important

later it had disappeared
from the table

I touch wet base
word blur
hart's tongue

bark bulge
above my head
                              a blown wall

but this is simply absorbed
no need for repair

the birds return
a flicker or a promise

you are standing still
ears exposed

hair marked
by lichen

the thinning skin
if it specks?
                    if it speaks

Tall Tree

for Susana Gardner

buzzard sweeps
between firs

this column of the past
become a Tall Tree
trail a smooth surface

this column of the past
has lost our label
feet and inches

(insert)

boys with an angle
hold forty five degrees
to the top of the tree

girls pace the spread
of bracken trace
its outline on the map

rake hailstones
and measure

( )

unfurl the ferns
these flag wavers
the birds *wheat rattle*
skin space woken

this column of the past
I am not   become
lichen   become   bark
teeth   edge   taken

her dream of broken teeth
was it his gap tooth   or
bite of trunk   inbitten
column   arctic   crevasse

brook   (break)
a water mark wast water
was is water o
(not end)   note and near

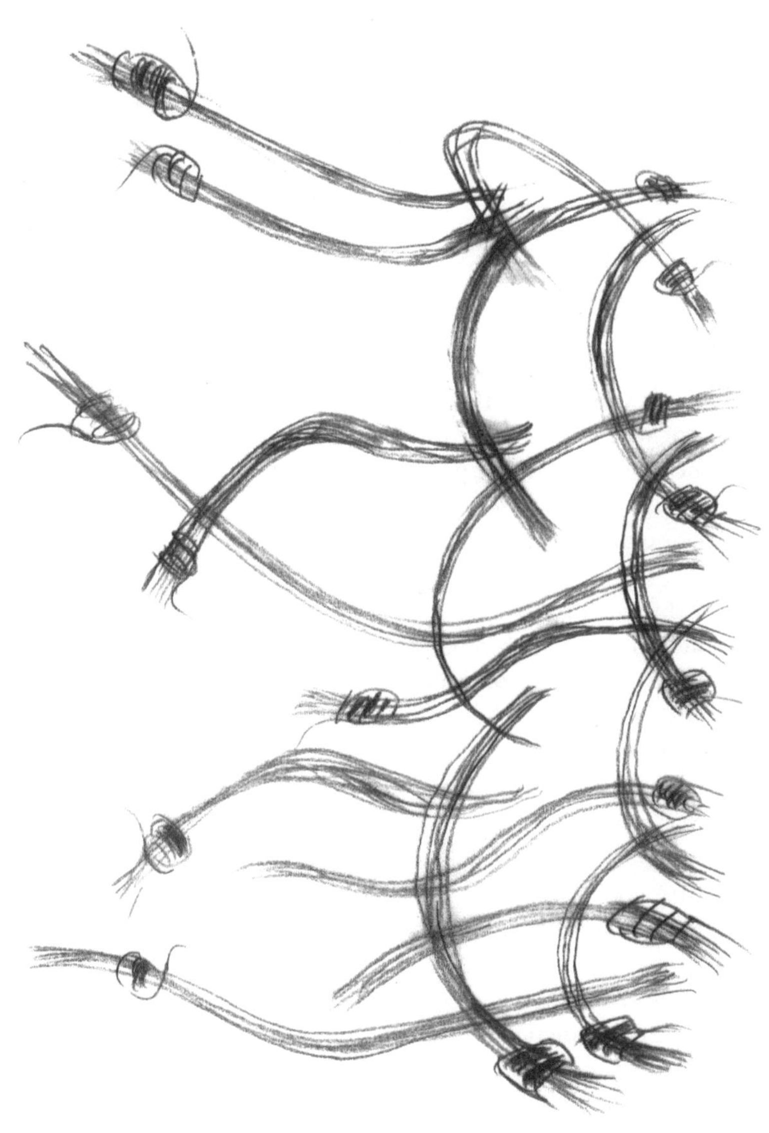

Lifting Lorna

close kernelling their blossom
were ruffled back
like a sleeve turned up
and nicked with brown at the corners

the hangers of the hazel
shrivelled at the base
and fell
as if a knife had cut them

I know not where the beginning was
nor where the middle ought to be
nor even how at the present time I feel
or think
or ought to think

I think
and nothing ever comes of it
nothing
which I can grasp
and have with any surety
nothing but faint images
and wandering

memory
like a scared wild bird
flies
or am I a child
chasing a flown cageling
who among the branches free
plays and peeps at the offered cage

black root-stuff was in her mouth
and a piece of dirty sheep's wool

Set beneath my chin
the veinings of a varnished buttercup

romancing gravely
playing at bo-peep with fear

a little figure
not insignificant (I mean)

You have not caught me yet altogether
and if you will only keep away
I shall like you more and more

worm-casts prickling
like women's combs

I try to be serious!
Although I am sure the situation
as the Counsellor always says
at the beginning of a speech
the situation
to say the least
is serious enough for anything

quick she had always been and *peart*
(as we say on Exmoor)
gifted with a leap of thought too swift for me to follow
hence you may find fault with much
when I report her sayings

I shall only be more timid
and more miserable
indoors

half the lattice was blocked up
as if plastered with grey lime
            in the only undarkened part
countless dots came swarming, clustering,
beating with a soft low sound
not as drops of rain do
but each distinct from its neighbour

            In our happy valley
            nine-tenths of what is said is false
            and you were always wont to argue
            true and false are but a blind
            turned upon a pivot

this long speech was too much for her
she had over-rated her strength about it
and the sustenance of irony

                        and that white sustenance

arrested

white
figure

small
veins
small
hands
little
feet
little
lamb
snow
y
twig

tim
id
taper
ing
not
in
sig
nif
icant
dear

quick
s
witch

peart
halse

Col

controlled burn

lost   cones   pine   burn

easier   to   fly

and   suspend

haunch   of   wood   charcoal

twigs   or   turning   forks

remaining   air

revolving   ogham

this is how we make our letters
first   we burn the tree

b eith   birch

l uis

blaze   n in

branch

emerging   fish   come to the surface

rising   to die

and falling

Yew man

Y – Yew man eating his hat – isolation
Lynette Roberts

pushed up push up
work it work it work it

got above himself
I ***am*** *the übermensch* you said

this is not true to the yew
here on the ground is dull grey green
feather leaves gentle on eyes

too cold to step out a roundel

here we go round
the mulberry bush the mulberry bush

so early cold and frosty morning
join hands and dance overcoats broken stove

inside the trunk her shrivelled form
holds up ancillary stack
as fern leaf sprouts on bark

van man has driven up the top
hat man so far up he has disappeared

rubbed by the friction of bird song
forcing thru pin holes
bird taps out finely drilled

he has pushed out pushed through
the top of his hat pierced drum

found air clearer a bald head
and light eternally wan

Borrowdale yews

I

yew sprouts feather grass green
            all along the branches
from inside the trunk

            branches fold through
                        fold down

light green on dark green
            new growth

in the river bed it survives
               on white stones

opposite
slabs of flood defence

only itself to anchor
not dislodged
or disbouldered

hear stream
            my bed is sound river

      drops vowels
                        yw

II

after Wordsworth

exposed white bark
white bone
starched shirt
pin stripe
o fraternity

wild oak

trunk may be

straight
crook
ed
cor~
k
scr~
w

epi
cormic
twigs
sprout through bark

grow in patches

fur   cover   the whole trunk

or absent

leaves open early
fall late

leafage   dense

or

sparse

birch migrating

uckoo
cuck   oo

turning away
is turning toward

birch migrated
turned several times
around itself

a forwarding and backwarding
a never quite finished

new growth where it had left off
sticks may be projected

rises from bogland
pitted by cattle

we would need to prune
when there is no need at all

it is another turning
a travel of leaves beyond

a form that is lifted and dropped

You were dark he said
I am fair

The resident poet was not at the pub

we do not migrate who most migrate

movement

for Anders

which leaves my body
bødy bådy
heavy on this stone

all we need for a table
            a flat slab
all we need for a cairn

the endless fall of notes

murrain
                              moraine

send fergal perambulation
in Norwish

whey which is not cheese
                but   far sweeter

Alison's last tapestry
                    fir trees
            half dark
                         half light

spots on her x-ray
showed the spread of cancer
but I still like my skeleton

birch twigs doused on the fire
tipping the tub over dissolving
bodies

because I am here
wondering what to wear
until I wear nothing
not even my glasses

dogs roll in the small drifts
the son who licks my sweat
he's a good licker

that was the joke
my title in translation

i mors liv
is not just 'in the life of my mother'
but could also mean 'womb'
she explained

and I wanted to explain that
'significant moments in the life of my mother'
avgjørende øyeblikk i mors liv
was meant to be absurd

an epic life
which has only two

eye
blinks

cycad

for Maria Irene Ramalho

cycad
cyclad
cyclop seed eye

sheds no leaves
grows slow
fossilising its torso

how did they uprise link arms and move their feet
how do they
unpopular
in a recession

does the madonna of the popular
spread her cape
in an earthquake
take them all under one wing

they must have missed him
stepping out of the tomb
his elegant foot
on a soldier's neck

no one can scale this tree
it has its own scales
it has shed letters

cycad pushes us back
the recess in a cave
which leads nowhere

a figure with a tail
drawn in the margin
curves us through

Jardim Botanico, Lisboa ~ 2010 ~ 1974 ~ 1755

palms

fibrous bark resists intruders
the reassuring brown of its shaved
planks scattered on the beach

bark scales are spouts on a church roof
/gargoyle pouts/ furtive overshoots retain moisture

the upper spouts are spiked
a carnivorous plant /or psyche/

the lower fronds are dry they are the shades
that turn our dreams to black and white
in a holiday camp we have never visited

a world of vibrant nurses and radiant uniforms
which we will never leave because we exist inside the box

they speak of silent love affairs among the dying
and a higher plane from which she returns with mother of pearl

the larger fronds have serrated edges
are chainsaws from a window display in Seljuk
they are not chainsaws they are all electric singing and dancing

Palm Sunday was never the yellow of these fronds
it's international yellow it's sunlight through slats
that never before saw sunlight they close in on themselves weeping

Syrian fronds that cannot rake an accidental shell

we do not want war
we do not seek war but we must defend our borders

do not pour water on my shell

OBX

one legged twisting god
Muriel Rukeyser: *Outer Banks*

1

trees which advance into the scrub zone are whipped
and sheared down to scrub size

one legged
scorched out
god

back flung
raised arms

black and white
fingers

tell them

tell them the letters

slash pitch

p ine

paper canoe

b irch

white bark
thin layers

a bird sits/
sat/ sits/
on a black white twig

wings fan

dac
tyl

dive

2

almost oak
almost live

backward branches
y'all come back

flung back her hair
her head

quercus virginiana

or not come back

how could they
with so little planning
no supplies

so little made
so little shaped
or turned

here we stood
here we stayed

here we cannot move
will not be moved

sealed we are sealed
in this great trunk

black stays
long severed branch

3

This beach called the swimming hole is between the aquarium and the regional airport. Poor specimens of trees with small branches and dead twigs. Leaves cluster for protection. I walk down what was the slipway of a seaplane, a gentle concrete slope into sand. An old wooden jetty falls and suspends. The long new bridge to the mainland. Shallow water dark with soil, grass and pine needles, which do not separate. Brackish. Steamrollers lay tarmac on the runway. No planes fly. Fed Ex is waiting. With loud beeps the steamroller reverses all the way to the fence. A black driver in a yellow fluorescent jacket stands up straight, opens his arms and shouts.

4

listen
listen to what I'm saying
>

she broke down and cried
is it ok to cry in the Senate?
she went missing
so you surprise people
we all know the buck stops with me
I messed up
I accepted responsibility
the State Department dropped the ball
big time
I would say she's the brains
>

it wasn't our business
you point a gun at me   I point a gun at you
out of control
the red line
they called that bluff
get over it
it's over with
that's my point
>

if we take this
if we take this
class system
break that down
>

when I get up at five in the morning
I'm looking at my pay check with no benefits
fighting a losing battle

pine remnant

stalks out
stakes out territory
substance   put out

all red brown found
roots rise ground

we do not bribe
are not bribed
we break   we coil

bark scale
age fissures
                                        U   U   U
weak stress

it says the river
it says a cloud of midges

held on a dead log
ferns

trying not to breathe
and still inhale

coille coire chuilc

                                        C   C   C

coille   wood
coire   cauldron
chuilc   reeds

hollow on hillside

do not appease
sharp quartz crystals

dislodge a boulder to roll

Atlantic hazel

hazel woods could be fitted to larger patterns
but I thought of them as lesser forms of something else
George Peterken

each small stick pushing up alongside
an older thicker stem
such large leaves already

uckoo   more insistent   uckoo
punctuates

continuity   of   wood   pigeon

blame it all on immigrants

a voice is coming through the wood

looking for this…
have you seen it?

she is looking for lost sheep
she is the farmer   she owns the land

played in these woods as children
it was more open then
now they allow it to grow and cover

follow the linear descent of bird song
splaying   lying

uckoo

shoot up from lichen tusks

you have to eliminate some of these stems
to make a drawing

they must be cut
must not be cut
cut into the form of
something else
the idea of a tree

Ballachuan
May 14

hassel

Oak change

The oak has changed its nature and this is called the Oak Change. Hitherto oaks had grown from seed within existing woods, but with few exceptions this ceased in the twentieth century. They were supposed to hold their own in the plot, as part of a densely worded argument and the interjection of many different, though similar, and invasive voices. Anything else was regarded as being contrary and self seeking. He had not noticed that methods of inscription had changed in the twentieth century, with the gradual elimination of the curving loop which led up to the first person pronoun. Oak now grows freely from acorn almost anywhere – heathland, farmland, railway land (although these anywheres are diminishing) – except within existing woods. Old photographs show a dense cluster of family members reliant on the spread skirt of the female lap, although some females sit perfectly upright. There is no trace of the adult males. This was the pattern he had wanted to recreate.

To sum up the main points of the argument, the oak changed its nature and this was not transcribed in his manual of fruit trees. It is disconcerting that a common tree should violate the Principle of Uniformity – that its present behaviour should furnish an interpretation of the past – and there has been much conjecture as to its cause. The most plausible reason is the introduction from America of oak mildew, a fungus disease first noticed in 1908 that rapidly spread to every deciduous oak in Europe.
The best of her men and most of her money had disappeared in the mud of Europe
The mildew has little effect on oaks growing in the open – but it may be death to an oakling in a wood struggling against shade.
My parents were not easily dismayed, I was their eighth offspring
In the next generation, however, there were principles which no longer seemed to apply, such as the assumed lack of communication between the male and its offspring.
We'll never rear them, mother

He may have had some awareness of the change, as he gestured at a clearing in the woods, and thought that most suitable for a sapling. The National Trust did not agree, although they rarely check the spread of sweet chestnut, laurel, rhododendron, and other opportunists, due to the absence of tied cottagers.

we deal with trees as actors in the play

that it should come to this, Horatio

their shades have become our anywhere

burnt tree / MT

Was it a healthy tree that someone burnt?

burnt out
broke through
harmless from any angle

(straight to camera)

never a hand to a face
never a smile to an eye
never a word to (re) read

seared the last tear
reduced to bone
reduced to ash

really tries to get her own way
by throwing a strop

charred bark
gone strip
took a rub a drub

strop strap
flayed bark
they were torn off a strip

she was silenced
on a bench
in the upper chamber

silenced by an absence
of counci(se)l

it goes lop   lop
arms are out   arms are cut
we are armed   alms are cut

burnt print

what will happen to health
services scattered

will turn into

private cherry-picking

up for grabs

to have remnants

a tongue tied tau(gh)t
by grammar
let our tongues
take truth
from this or any other *place*

what would
English music
have been like if

our descant
on the stairs

the choir is singing
a capella pieces
from the golden

be in my head
be in my eyes
be in my mouth
be in my heart

at my end
and at my departing

burnt root

WHITE BIRCH

WHITE ASH

WHITE CIDER

WHITE ICE

SILVER

London
April 13

Hatfield forest

for Peter Philpott

missed mistle
oak   on the shore
line   spread out
your toes   press down
these joins   are still in use

and now the roar   and now the roar
an aeroplane and   then another   and another
and then air o   air a   plane and a plane and other planes

skim round   or wait   motionless
a stack   of geese   keep circling
or rising   insatiable   hoor   shore

thorn thrust
inside   the oak
it comes in   the thorn
crosses   old   branches

lie   lie   lie   sleeping banks
let   lulled   too   lie
allow   the   murmur
the   murmurous   shore   of propulsion

I'm big mummy duck   *Stink, you swim in your own shit*
Look at the dirty big animal

they fly in their own

white foot raised above the water

silver

candle lit with an IOU
the impot
            of the import

stone columns
upright in the light
cannot sustain

white flash of a tree
distortion from diamond panes

a series of stills
a film which consists of

constant movement in the branches

silver birch
dying at the top

a gawky splay
and still though louder

the white butterfly climbs

patches of grey near the base
peel away

skin peeling is wrong

gated ~~communities~~
estates
are wrong

hello, he said
clinging to the pram
hello lady
gor geous

convolvulus has place here
is whiter than the skin of birch
gorgeous convolvulus

inside the cell
my credit flames

Julian's garden
Norwich

hesil nutt

'he shewed a littil thing, the quantitye of an hesil nutt'
Julian of Norwich

no fear of credit
in this our birth year

light two candles

I'm gonna be   I'm gonna be
reclaim that energy

for here
the lilies
before the peace

What is happening to my body

something found in the seaweed
a dip in the brain
concave lights

his nut brown pate
his hazelnut

uncovered always open
to wind   and rain   and sun

he does not doff his cap
or bow

hazel is the head
no skull   memento mori

two candles burn low
in plastic containers

light filled

empty

dotterel

I

automatic shots lobbed
                              over tree tops
pop pop   pop
          clay or Clare shooting

grau   grau   grau   wood
pigeons   the lower register
finds a comfort and authority

clouds part for deepest   jet
bass   boom
pointed wings
                                    sharp nose

sends   whirra   whirra   whirra
of descending wing

Royce wood
gone tangle
shoots shot through

conifer beech ash
fallen with tight plaiting
of honeysuckle

this is not our nursery
nor conifers our nurse

these trees crash in
there is a pressure
an assault
saulted

II

I am not stulped
but bounced
on broken trunk
snapped off to sawdust base

white twine
red berries
bitter   sweet   byrony

wind wood anemones
blown together
by washed out plastic sacks

stems arched
rerouted
routed

and still they sing
my understorey
invisible in the thicket

their wasteful hoping and looping
smallest of small survivors
faireys for the boys

~~Ann Yearsley~~ struggles into voice

cut out
and put in his scrap

she could dot you one as good as any lad

dot   dot   dot   dotter

dotterel

Percevall wood

bark break   fragment
or slow   space

bark blocks   separate   out
          molton wax
laced haste

up come   up pluck   up string
between one conifer   and the next
up take   a crowded leaning or leading

leaves shine undercover
underleaf

what is their capacity for work?

re-establish the balance
of broadleaves and conifers

make them lift their arms
in three different positions

heavy with beech leaves

the intermediate is the most difficult
an interrogation

or broken with pine cones

but then it's not about the function
it's about how you use the arm

the lift of sycamore

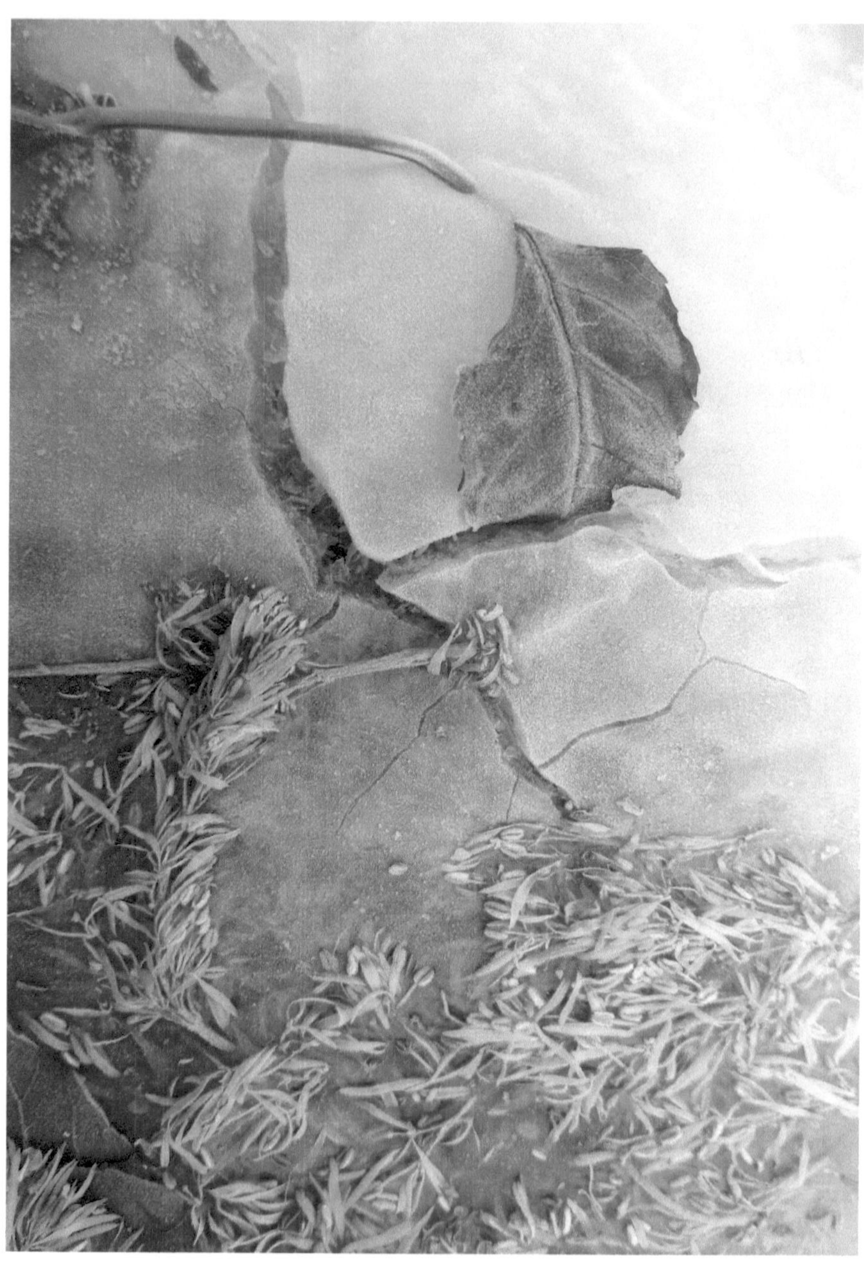

branches

for Carol Watts

funnelled through the tunnel between the crowding trees
rook scrapes the bark does beak clean birch or is it just
building a hole? the whole vista reduced cut in two
threaded by telegraph wires small brown bird wobbles
totters blackbird grabs orange berries gr(o)aps vertical
ascent everything has to be ascending the copper of the
copper beech dries my eyes if you weight a branch with
feeding last night I dreamt she held a box of toys
small figures connected by pipe cleaners which could be
twisted in various directions the mother and child agree
that these could be thrown away everybody has a hung
hung hungry heart

white lift
underside of ash

the trunk has breaches
bird calls and response

if if if
what what what
so so so

tree shadow on tarmac
tower bridge within sight of
I could not work

the strait is always the strait
and he did not know why
she chose the narrow gate

these towers hold branches in suspension

si   si   si
seep   seed

no visible structure on Robberby road
shadow puppets   connectives
cut out

ash hanging

shreds of shreds
some attachment

green ribbon floats
in the wind
is not the colour to choose
if you wish to be visible

red ribbon
that strip rarely used
jumps up above the keys
tugging off the spool

the fullness of a ribbon
bowed red in the sun

fray ed threads
are not for letters

what does each attachment mean?

bandaged branch

shredded black cloth
scanty covering
just his trunks
to bear him up
in the air
too exposed   the soft flesh

he is dangling
never knew his father
a grey trunk
was the dangling man

words
on a key ring
too high to read

hanging gold discs
with ribbons and feather

transparent plastic discs
on little metal rings

hollow green discs
ready for a mix
ready for a short song

pocket of keys
purse of seeds
of brown gold coins   a shower

the gusset hanging
quested   guessed

Long Meg
Cumbria
June

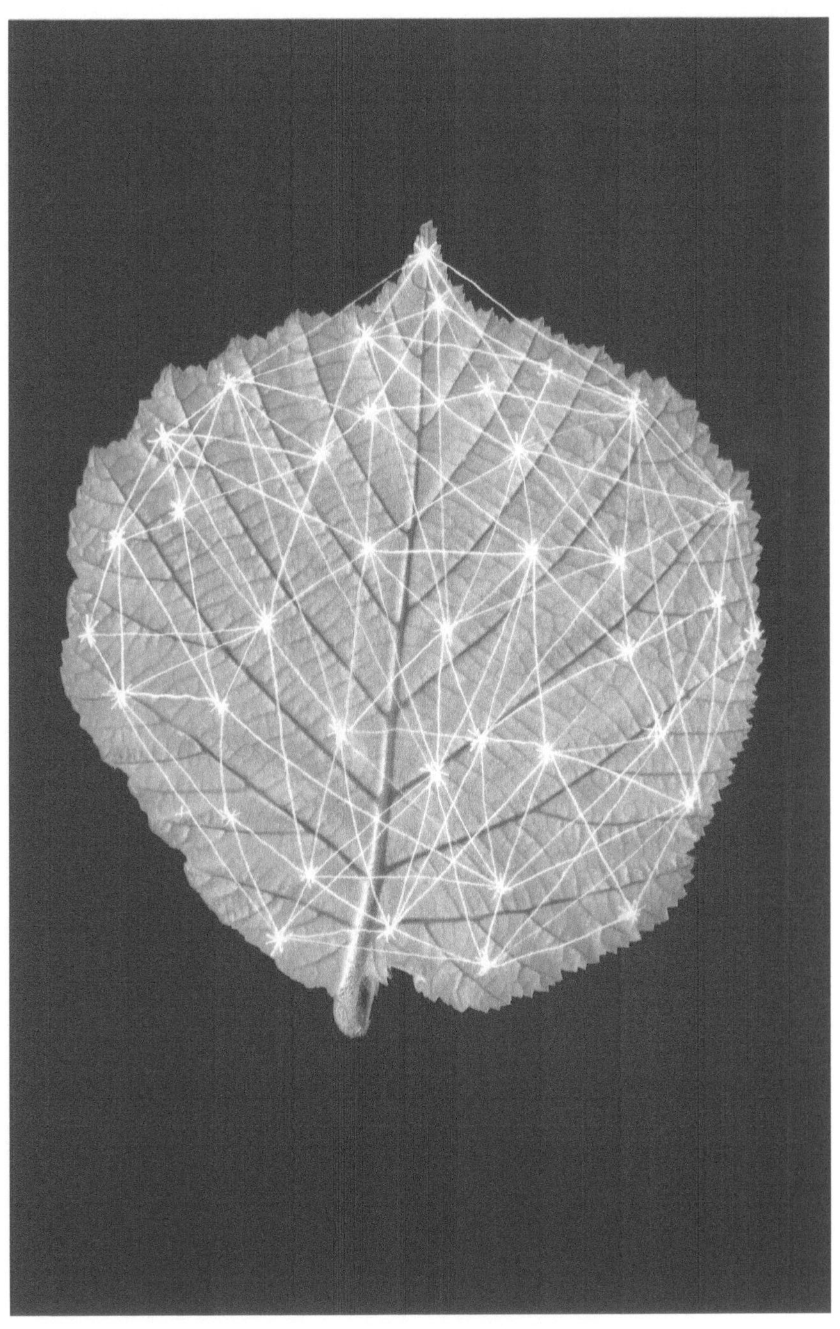

leaf notes

Common whitebeam
        curled up leaf
        lacking chromosomes
white underneath

'Grey-leaved' whitebeam
  bright green   sharp teeth   point out
                                          prow

Bristol whitebeam   teeth
                                  climb
                                      steps

Leigh Woods whitebeam
                         in the teeth
                           of her white lace collar

Cheddar whitebeam

        pinstripe veins

            translucent against light

English whitebeam

          feathery side veins

                dark against the light

leaf retina

some account of the art of laser radiation, or the process by which the eye may be made to delineate itself without the aid of the artist's pencil

when the light comes in it is green green green
very light bright green
the green of new spring leaves seen though vinyl
and the veins on the leaves ar your own veins
your blod vessels
it also turns to yellow a bright yellow
and then finally into the stratosphere the stars

through a glass the shows the glass into shoves the glass into
the wrong end of the telescope
this light pulses into your brain
in schock waves
bores its way into your head to seal a tear or two
tears

to stop you from seeing nothing from seeing
white flasing lights
or a series of flating of dark of smudge of soot
os speck of soot on the leaf of maybe moth of maybe flight

the eye is watching the eye retains the retina
retains the veins the imprint
the print is too bright it is tiger green
the eye is dispersing pierced persant pursuant

of fluying things methough I saw
methought it would clear
there is no clarity at most a bright and fringed light
at most green leaf painted with a roller
it is the perfect symmetry veins veins like field notes

....

Most of the cameraless photogenic drawings record ferns, grasses
and leaves. Fox Talbot suggested in one of his letters that naturalists
would find the accurate recording of botanical specimens to be among
the most important uses of his invention, especially when the photogenic
drawings were made through a solar microscope.
Very fine details of leaf structure are clearly visible in several

the retina is the layer of neurosensory tissue that lines the
back wall of the eye   if you imagine that your eye is a camera
the retina   is   the film   as a picture cannot be developed
if the camera   has defective film
vision is not possible   in an eye   with a defective retina

Atwood afterleaf

Martha Atwood's whitebeam
her original gathering:
10 June 1852

This tree on a separate ridge of rocks
struck the eye immediately as distinct in appearance

label shows her critical acumen:
many annotations show difficulties later caused

now named Bristol whitebeam: sorbus Bristoliensis

Miss Martha Maria Atwood at her microscope:
1856 (a bad year):
small photograph found in Bristol Flora

gloss coil hair
black dress white lace collar

eye in shadows
light on long nose
index finger
and lens

silver pin holes fox the image

she identifies eyebright

whitebeam prow

slim trunk
keep anchor
clipped under

extend twigs
form fruit
at furthest reach

follow the contour of the cliff
however you need to get there
do not stop her

and move with lesions
with lenticels

edible as we are
eyed fruit
semicircle of rain
dark spots on red berries

scratched across
script
markings on bark

slow stretch of sorbus
outpace
slow heave of carriage
for care

knot ripples
ride the tide

the tree is leading the tree over the gorge

<sorbus porrigentiformis>
Avon Gorge, October

Ribs and leaves

a collaboration with Julia Cohen

You lived in a house drawn
from pencils

we live in a terrace re
assembled from London stocks

An unregulated minute
You turn your apples to bones

the pitch of a public address
bathes children in tarmac

We learn to digest.
We learn organism.
At night babies are delivered.
Shake the immense reciprocal.

we earn to ingest
we earn orgasms
at night holes in the wall are reloaded
counterfeit the global exchange

You are a balcony blistering
with rain. A handshake extended
as a noose.

we pitch the whole pencil
through the paper-like face
of tripped minutes

JC/FP

acid grassland

rotted birch trunks
waves of yellow fungus
this is edge

of a thicket guilty
with solar clods
or lunch kneeling over

scent flicks tail
tongue sticks out
grey body close

what's left behind
enjambs the freckled twigs

to snag the washed-out foil
and wrappers, graceless with sheen

they have built a hedge to stop the slope
the embankment
parallel staves
dead branches between

joggers and hoodies
slip slide
to hide
to hide a rise
which is fair for all

fair for all to see

sheep's sorrel
mouse-ear hawkweed
small skipper butterfly

mining bees burrow tiny holes in the ground

FP/JC

Glazed Leaf

your house hung on a branch
you doled out the moss impetus
a partial field cracked on the teeth
the hammock to catch what?

this house hangs on an amphitheatre
a dropped coin catches the gallery
a complete fist cracks on your teeth
she once attempted a hammock

mixing or glazing them I lowered
your shoulders
to be at ease, one's own

finding and cutting above the eye
to turn it outwards
is still a possible growth

you unclogged the incipient cloud
teething cumulous, your glowing
tendrils, you heavily fructified

two red contrails converge
an acute angle in the evening sky
private debt becomes public
loss, like a lake exploding with leaves

JC/FP

from the bridge

an arm reaches down
bronze and ivy
a hand on the bricks
ivy leaves separate around the fingers

clutch the mould clutch
your lip lined with the loss of
tides

bridge leaves
rivets
leaf mould in metal
gone at gone over
new earth
new loss
grey membrane peels
to red underlayer

THiS iS FoR
All THe loST
LoVeD oNeS
RIP
RoeNA

hawks and spits
buddleia
gathers pace

economically inactive
the green shoots of

you take the train to tarnish
the leaf-blower's job
HeLLO, this is
the fort priced for an ivy reach

gold leaf sprays
on a tag

KeS   TABoo

the greening edge of parallel platforms

FP/JC

DUPLO

bricks grow
out of roots, something
like a snowball

thrown through
the red floor
its brief curling

NORA DUPLO

the houses, the houses
bleach to meet
our clouds

headless the mannequin
torso touching
our ground

in the birdcage sits
a filmy jug and my fingers
stained with beets

my feet squirrel proof
the song cage
such lasts   such lasts   such lasts   to lead

if you took the truculent
branch, if we used our hands
to dig

if you invent the lettered
fork   if we pierce
the bed

JC/FP

Archway tunnel

metal grids guard the entrance
once we could walk through
precise brick geometry
the blues

once we bricked once we
stepped over the blue
no octagon stops the city
sitting in ivy

an elongated carnivorous mouth
something monstrous
not a monstrance
mister across the teeth **MR**
m is an orifice

the office of dried twigs
administration of feather
& gravel

the tunnel protects
deposits of dead leaves
brambles
shambles
cur-cur cur cur-cur
wood pigeons

are we waiting on the wind?
nothing kempt
the air a little greyer than your
eyes

thin birch trunks
bent over
swathed in ivy
over and over
this great garment
wild berried
is not too much to bear

if we took to learn? if we took to
stain our thumbs.

FP/JC

March 11

Notes

halse

p.15 'The Forest of Exmoor was such a wild wind-swept waste that a single tree was a notable landmark; and on the old commons outside the royal game-preserve, where the land was a little easier, tree names still recall lost woodlands and old ways of life'. 'Oak, ash and thorn' Hazel Eardley-Wilmot, *Exmoor Review*, 25, 1984, pp. 43-44.

p.17 Landed families planted trees and shaped the woods, and had permission from the Crown to 'impark' land as private game preserves. 'There are no finer oaks than the splendid old trees in Nettlecombe Deer Park… some of them still stand, looking remarkably vigorous with girths of 15 feet or more.' Roger Miles, *The Trees and Woods of Exmoor,* Exmoor Press, 1972.

p.18 Bampfylde Clump, also known as the Round Ring, is a plantation of beech trees above North Molton. 'The outstanding change came in mid-century with the enclosure of the commons. On the Bampfylde/ Poltimore land, cultivation crept steadily uphill, field by geometrical field'. Hazel Eardley-Wilmot, *Yesterday's Exmoor*, Exmoor Books, 1990.

p.19 Burnt mounds, made of charcoal and stone fragments, are evidence of very early methods of heating water for communal purposes.

p.20 'Of all the boundary marks of the old deer forest of Exmoor the most famous is a tree. The Hoar Oak Tree has marked for centuries the forest edge… several saplings were planted in 1916… one remains, struggling bravely within iron railings against a hostile climate. Although over 50 years old, the trunk diameter is scarcely more than a hand's span'. Roger Miles, *ibid.*

p.21 'If any one tree can be described as the oldest vegetable in the Exmoor region, it is probably the Flitton Oak. On the OS maps the tree is indicated with old English lettering… it may be some ancient boundary mark. It is a pollard and hollow… it cannot be dated: the heartwood has rotted'. Roger Miles, *ibid.*

p. 25 Hazel Eardley-Wilmot *Yesterday's Exmoor*, *ibid.*
March Against the Cuts, 2011.

p.29 A collection of Douglas firs was planted in 1874 on the Dunster Castle estate, and now includes the tallest tree in England. It has become a tree trail with information boards. *Dunster Forest Tall Trees Trail,* Crown Estate www.thecrownestate.co.uk

p.32 R. D. Blackmore, *Lorna Doone: a romance of Exmoor*, 1869. This poem was originally part of a sequence on statues of women in public spaces (see *Lines of Sight*, 2009). There is a statue of Lorna outside the Exmoor National Park office in Dulverton.

p.39 From a Cornelia Parker mobile, 'Heart of darkness', made of pieces of charred wood from a forest fire. Ogham is an early mediaeval alphabet, resembling Germanic runes, inscribed on monuments. It is sometimes called the 'Celtic tree alphabet' after a High Mediæval Briatharogam tradition ascribing names of trees to the individual letters. This was pursued by Robert Graves in *The White Goddess: a historical grammar of poetic myth,* Faber, 1961.

p.40 'The theme (of the poem) is both of words and alphabet all of which is based on the true symbols – letters and psychological meanings transferred and brought up to date without checking the original symbol or meaning from the text. I took the key from our friend the Rev Mr Davies an eg is Y – Yew man eating his hat – isolation. I think this is funny!! The Ego or superego man & then the madness tailing off'. Lynette Roberts to Robert Graves, Dec 13th 1943.

Lynette Roberts: Diaries, letters and recollections ed. Patrick McGuinness, Carcanet, 2008. Roberts helped Graves with his research for *The White Goddess*, but did not take sources such as the Rev Mr Davies as seriously as he did. I also used Roberts' essay *Village Dialect*, Druid Press, 1944.

p.41 After Wordsworth's 'The Yew Trees' (1803) and his 'fraternal Four of Borrowdale'. Later I discovered that the three surviving ancient yews are female: 'The Borrowdale yews, Taxus baccata L: the 'Fraternal Four' near Seathwaite, Borrowdale', by Toby Hindson, 2012.

p.44 From Oliver Rackham's *Woodlands*, Harper Collins, 2006.

p.45 'One birch tree is literally migrating across the site in a windward direction and where one veteran birch has fallen, eight healthy trees have been created as branches have converted to trunks'. *Geltsdale's wood pasture*, by Martin Clark, East Cumbria, 2008.

p.51 Muriel Rukeyser *Outer Banks*, Unicorn, 1967. *Seacoast plants of the Carolinas*, Karl E Graetz, North Carolina University Press, 1973.

p.57 *The Ancient pinewoods of Scotland: a traveller's guide*, Clifton Bain, Sandstone, 2013.

p.58 *Atlantic hazel: Scotland's special woodlands*, Sandy and Brian Coppins, Atlantic Hazel Action Group, 2012. Forward by George Peterken.

Sarah Simblet on her drawings for a contemporary version of John Evelyn's *Sylva*: *The New Sylva* by Gabriel Hemery and Sarah Simblet, Sylva Foundation, 2014.

pp.63-4 From Oliver Rackham's *Woodlands*, ibid. The italics are my father's words and sayings.

pp.65-7 On the day of Margaret Thatcher's funeral. 'Let our tongues...', 'Veras hinc ducere voces' (Virgil, *Aeneid*), Grantham Girls' Grammar School motto. 'God be in my head', Sarum Primer, 1558.

p.69 'The best preserved of all Forests is Hatfield, Essex'. *The history of the countryside*, by Oliver Rackham, Dent, 1986. Rackham also mentions a disused airfield, now Stansted airport.

p.72 *A Revelation of Love*, by Julian of Norwich, ed. Marion Glasscoe, University of Exeter, 1993.

p.73 Royce (Rice) wood, Helpston. Dotterel is a pollarded tree and stulp is a tree stump. Glossary, *John Clare*, ed. Eric Robinson and David Powell, Oxford University Press, 1984. '"The Woodman" and the Natural Anthology' by Paul Chirico, *John Clare Society Journal*, 19, July 2000, pp. 41-51.

p.75 Percevall Hall in the Yorkshire Dales, run by the Diocese of Bradford. Quotations in italics are about the new tests to assess disability benefits. 'The folk at ATOS who carry out the work capability assessment frequently miss out the question about the intermediate arm position, probably the most difficult one to sustain, and I gather it was used in Northern Ireland during interrogations of IRA suspects' (Bruce Barnes).

pp.79-80 Long Meg is a Neolithic stone circle in Cumbria where an ash tree is decorated in mid-summer. Another 'dangling man' can be found in Norse legend: Yggdrasil is the tall tree whose roots go far down below the earth and it can also be Odin's horse or gallows. The *Poetic Edda* describes how Odin sacrifices himself to himself by hanging from a tree, and is saved by the runes. (Transl. Gavin Selerie, *Azimuth*, Binnacle Press, 1984, and *Technicians of the Sacred*, ed. Jerome Rothenberg, University of California Press, 1985).

p.82 From notes on whitebeam leaves collected from Avon and Cheddar Gorges by Libby Houston. A rare whitebeam is named after her: *sorbus houstoniae*. See *Whitebeams, rowans and service trees of Britain and Ireland*, by Rich, Houston, Robertson and Proctor, BSBI, 2010.

p.83 An experience of laser eye surgery for a damaged retina at Moorfields Eye Hospital. Henry Fox Talbot, photography pioneer: 'Some account of the art of photogenic drawing, or the process by which natural objects may be made to delineate themselves without the aid of the artist's pencil' (1839).

p.85 'Martha Atwood', by Clive Lovatt, *Bristol Naturalists Society*, 468, March 2008.

Ribs and leaves

pp.87-98 This collaboration was commissioned by David Hawkins and Caleb Klaces, editors of the website *Likestarlings*, www.likestarlings.com. The normal format is a short exchange of poems, but Julia and I decided to intervene in each other's texts. The poems I initiated were written on the 'Parkland Walk', not a parkland at all, but a disused railway line in north London and now an urban nature reserve. About halfway through we also decided to exchange images: it was not possible to include all of them here, so I have chosen two examples.

Acknowledgements

Poems have appeared in the following journals and anthologies and I would like to thank all the editors concerned: *Molly Bloom,* Aiden Semmens, www.mollybloompoetry.weebly.com; *Long Poem Magazine*, Linda Black and Lucy Hamilton; *Osiris*, Andrea Moorhead; *Pinstripe Fedora*, Jane Nakagawa; *Poetry Review*, Fiona Sampson; *Poetry Wales,* Zoë Skoulding; *Shearsman,* Tony Frazer; *The Volta*, Jessica Smith, www.thevolta.org.

Salamanders & Mandrake: Gavin Selerie and Alan Halsey at Sixty, ed. David Annwn, Is Press, 2009; *As linguas da poesia: the tongues of poetry: 7th International Meeting of Poets*, Faculty of Letters, University of Coimbra, Portugal 2010; *Entanglements: anthology of ecopoetry*, ed. Sharon Blackie and David Knowles, Two Ravens, 2012; *The Other Room Anthology 6*, ed. James Davies, Tom Jenks and Scott Thurston, Manchester: Other Room, 2014; *Fit to Work: poets against ATOS* http://ftwpoetsagainstatos.wordpress.com 2013.

The poem 'Halse' is available as a Five Seasons Broadside, designed by Glenn Storhaug. www.fiveseasonspress.com

'Oak change' appeared in 'Time the deer is in the wood of Hallaig', an exhibition curated by Amy Cutler: http://amycutler.wordpress.com/2013/05/14/time-the-deer-is-in-the-wood-of-hallaig-6-11th-june

I have many people to thank for their help with research, walks and hospitality, especially Anders, Bruce Barnes, Hanne Bramness, Clive Bush, Caroline Cornish, Amy Cutler, Lyn Davies, Jane Freshwater, Barbara and Tom Hall, Penny Hallas, Graham Hartill, Libby Houston, Janet and David Jenkins, Owain Jones, Joy Leach, George MacLennan, Chris Ozzard, Peter Philpott, Anna Reckin, Lucy Sheerman, Zoe Skoulding, Harriet Tarlo, Alexandra Trowbridge-Mathews and, always, my partner Gavin.

I am grateful to the Arts Council for a grant to enable me to complete this book.

www.ingramcontent.com/pod-product-compliance
Ingram Content Group UK Ltd.
Pitfield, Milton Keynes, MK11 3LW, UK
UKHW040559210726
13854UKWH00008B/1546

9 781848 613409